A Crabtree Branches Book

Today's Stars

SERENA WILLIAMS

Ellen Rodger

Crabtree Publishing
crabtreebooks.com

School-to-Home Support for Caregivers and Teachers

This high-interest book is designed to motivate striving students with engaging topics while building fluency, vocabulary, and an interest in reading. Here are a few questions and activities to help the reader build upon his or her comprehension skills.

Before Reading:

- *What do I think this book is about?*
- *What do I know about this topic?*
- *What do I want to learn about this topic?*
- *Why am I reading this book?*

During Reading:

- *I wonder why...*
- *I'm curious to know...*
- *How is this like something I already know?*
- *What have I learned so far?*

After Reading:

- *What was the author trying to teach me?*
- *What are some details?*
- *How did the photographs and captions help me understand more?*
- *Read the book again and look for the vocabulary words.*
- *What questions do I still have?*

Extension Activities:

- *What was your favorite part of the book? Write a paragraph on it.*
- *Draw a picture of your favorite thing you learned from the book.*

TABLE OF CONTENTS

GAME CHANGER

Not many people can say they are a game changer. But Serena Williams can. She is known as the greatest women's tennis player of all time, as well as one of the world's greatest athletes.

Serena has smashed records and boundaries in sports and life. She is not only a professional tennis champion, but also a respected businessperson and **philanthropist**.

Serena has won a record 23 **Grand Slam** women's **singles** tennis titles. She has changed how women's tennis is played and how it looks.

Serena loves fashion, on and off the court. She blazed a trail for bright, cool, and funky tennis wear.

Fun Facts

Serena and her older sister Venus grew up playing tennis. The Williams sisters both became top professional players.

A STAR IS BORN

Serena Jameka Williams was born on September 26, 1981, in Saginaw, Michigan. Her parents, Richard Williams and Oracene Price, raised Serena and her **siblings** in Compton, California.

Serena, Richard, and Venus Williams

Serena's parents decided early on that she and her sister Venus would be tennis champs. They moved the family to West Palm Beach, Florida, when Serena was nine. There, Serena and Venus attended a leading tennis **academy**.

Serena has said that her tennis career wouldn't have been possible without her parents.

As top junior players, the Williams sisters dominated the courts. By the time Serena was in high school, Richard Williams had become a full-time coach for both his daughters.

Richard Williams hadn't played tennis before becoming a coach for his daughters. He taught himself the sport by watching instructional videos.

Fun Facts

Serena grew up with Venus and three older half-sisters, Yetunde, Lyndrea, and Isha Price.

MAKING WAVES

Serena entered her first professional tournament in 1995. She lost in the first round. She then focused on her education and training and did not play another professional match until two years later.

As both their coach and father, Richard wanted to make sure Serena and Venus were healthy, well-rounded individuals. He let them be kids. Richard also pushed them to learn both physical skills and emotional control.

Over the course of their professional tennis careers, Serena and Venus played against each other in 31 singles matches.

When Serena re-entered professional play, she began defeating older, more experienced players. She quickly rose in tennis **rankings**. In 1999, she won her first professional singles title.

Serena's strength and quick footwork made her a powerful competitor on the court.

Fun Facts

Richard Williams and Oracene Price studied all aspects of tennis before enrolling their daughters in lessons and coaching them.

QUEEN SERENA

Over the course of her professional tennis career, Serena broke records and won many awards. In 2019, she was named the Female Athlete of the Decade for the 2010s by the Associated Press.

Serena's many achievements include six U.S. Open women's singles titles.

Serena won 23 Grand Slam women's singles titles. She is the only woman to have done this in the current era of professional tennis.

Serena often played against her sister Venus in singles matches. Together, they also formed one of the most unbeatable doubles in tennis history. They won 14 Grand Slam doubles titles. Both earned the rank of world number one in singles.

Although the Williams sisters were very competitive when they played each other, they were still very close outside of tennis.

In addition to professional tennis, Serena competed in four Olympic Games. She won gold in doubles at the Sydney 2000 games and Beijing 2008 games. In London 2012, she won gold in both singles and doubles.

Serena is one of only three women to have won gold medals in both singles and doubles tennis at the same Olympic Games.

It has not always been easy for Serena. She suffered physical injuries and battled **anxiety** and depression while playing top-level tennis. Since having her children, however, Serena has worked hard to try to overcome her mental health challenges.

By talking publicly about her anxiety and depression, Serena has inspired other athletes to speak out about their own mental health challenges.

Fun Facts

Serena won the 2017 Australian Open while pregnant with her first child, Alexis Olympia! Her second child, Adira River, was born in 2023. Serena is married to billionaire Alexis Ohanian.

Serena retired from professional tennis in 2022, but she remains one of the best female tennis players of all time. On court, Serena was **ferocious** and strong physically and mentally. She fought for each game, set, and match.

The Williams sisters inspired many young Black tennis players, including Coco Gauff (left), to follow in their footsteps.

Serena was known for her powerful, focused playing style. Her incredibly fast serve allowed her to control play. It made it difficult for those who played against her to read what she would do next.

Serena was never afraid to challenge ***umpires*** *and officials if she felt they made a bad call.*

BUSINESS LEADER

Richard Williams got his daughters involved in tennis because he knew it was one sport where women could make a lot of money. Today, Serena and Venus are number one and two in all-time career prize earnings in tennis.

Serena and Venus own part of the Miami Dolphins NFL team.

Serena has used her wealth and fame to start and help other businesses. She founded a company called Serena Ventures that **invests** in companies that support **diversity**.

One of Serena's goals is boosting women and Black-owned businesses.

Serena created the Yetunde Price Resource Center to honor the life of her older sister who was killed in an act of violence. The center helps people heal from **trauma**.

Yetunde Price was the oldest of Serena's four sisters.

As a Black female leader, Serena has the power to influence others. She has joined with and funded charities that promote education, help victims of domestic abuse, and fight for justice.

Serena is a role model who believes it is important to teach kids that there are no limits.

Serena Williams changed the sport of tennis with her strong, fierce style of play. Throughout her life she has been a fighter, passionate about both her sport and helping others.

Serena has always been serious about winning, but she also has a great sense of humor.

Fun Facts

In between playing tennis, Serena attended fashion school and launched a fashion line. In 2023, she was the first athlete to receive the Council of Fashion Designers of America Fashion Icon award.

GLOSSARY

academy (uh-KAD-uh-mee): A school for special training or instruction

anxiety (ang-ZAHY-i-tee): A mental health condition that causes distress and uneasiness

diversity (dahy-VUR-si-tee): The state of having people in a group who have a variety of differences, including race, gender, and ethnicity

ferocious (fuh-ROH-shuhs): Fierce and intense

Grand Slam (grand slam): A term used to describe the world's four most important tennis championships that are played each year: the Australian Open, the French Open, Wimbledon, and the U.S. Open

invest (in-VEST): To put money and/or time into something that will pay off

philanthropist (fi-LAN-thruh-pist): A person who has concern for other people and shows it by donating money, time, or work to support organizations that serve the public

rankings (RANG-kings): Official positions or standings

siblings (SIB-lings): Sisters or brothers

singles (SING-guhls): A tennis match played with one person on each side

trauma (TRAW-muh): A long-lasting emotional response to a terrible event

umpires (UHM-pahyuhrs): People who rule on the plays of a game

INDEX

WEBSITES TO VISIT

https://www.serenawilliams.com

https://www.wtatennis.com/players/230234/serena-williams

https://www.womenshistory.org/education-resources/biographies/serena-williams

ABOUT THE AUTHOR

Ellen Rodger won a bank-sponsored short story contest at age nine. It was the last thing her bank ever gave her for free, but it kicked-started a career in newspaper, magazine, and book publishing. Ellen has written hundreds of books for curious young people, on topics as varied as the history of the potato, urban wildlife, refugees, the Great Lakes, and explorers.

Crabtree Publishing

crabtreebooks.com 800-387-7650

Written by: Ellen Rodger
Designed by: Kathy Walsh
Series Development: James Earley
Editor: Melissa Boyce
Educational Consultant: Marie Lemke M.Ed.
Production manager: Candice Campbell

Hardcover: 978-1-0398-8038-2
Paperback: 978-1-0398-8398-7
Ebook (pdf): 978-1-0398-8158-7
Epub: 978-1-0398-8278-2

Printed in the U.S.A./CP2025

Published in Canada
Crabtree Publishing
616 Welland Ave.
St. Catharines, Ontario
L2M 5V6

Published in the United States
Crabtree Publishing
347 Fifth Ave
Suite 1402-145
New York, NY 10016

Library and Archives Canada Cataloguing in Publication
Available at Library and Archives Canada

Library of Congress Cataloging-in-Publication Data
Available at the Library of Congress

Photographs
Alamy: Album p 8
Newscom: Kyodop 21, Splash News p 26
Shutterstock: Dorothy Hong, cover, title page, TOC, p 4, p 31; Leonard Zhukovsky, p 5, p 6, p 7 (top), p 16, p 17, p 22 (top), p 23, p 27; Jimmie48 Photography, p 7 (bottom), p 20, p 28; Phil Anthony, p 10 (top), p 14; Stuart Slavicky, p 10 (bottom); Everett Collection, p 11 (top), p 13; FlashStudio, p 11 (bottom); Neale Cousland, p 18 (top); Featureflash Photo Agency, p 18 (bottom); Colin McPhedran, p 22 (bottom); Gregory Reed, p 24 (bottom); dennizn, p 25; DFree, p 29
Wikimedia Commons: Creative Commons, p 9, p 12, p 19 (bottom), p 24 (top)
All other images from Shutterstock